SCHÜLER **Lernkrimi Englisch**

Danger Down Under

Gina Billy

W0085323

Vokabeltraining inklusive!

Lerne die Vokabeln zum Buch - mit phase6,
Deutschlands führendem Vokabeltrainer.*

www.phase6.de/s/a3174

Die Nr. 1 unter den Vokabeltrainern

© Circon Verlag GmbH
Baierbrunner Str. 27, 81379 München
Ausgabe 2022

Redaktion: Isabella Bergmann
Fachkorrektur: Nathalie Russell
Produktion: Ute Hausleiter
Titelillustration: oneinchpunch/shutterstock.com
Umschlaggestaltung und Gestaltung: red.sign GbR, Stuttgart

ISBN 978-3-8174-4259-1
38174259/1

Besucht uns auf Instagram und Facebook: circonverlag

www.circonverlag.de

Hello,

du willst dein Englisch verbessern und echte Lernerfolge haben? Dabei sollen Spannung und Spaß nicht zu kurz kommen? Dann ist dieses Buch genau das richtige für dich.

Dieser Schüler Lernkrimi basiert auf dem didaktischen Konzept unserer beliebten Compact Lernkrimis. Er kombiniert eine spannende Geschichte, abwechslungsreiche Übungen, Tipps zu Sprachgebrauch und Grammatik sowie viele Infos zu Land und Leuten.

Kurze Texteinheiten, Vokabelangaben auf jeder Seite und die langsame Steigerung des Niveaus stellen sicher, dass du beim Lernen optimal unterstützt wirst. Im Final Check kannst du deine Fortschritte überprüfen. So ist dieses Buch perfekt, wenn du ergänzend zum Schulunterricht deine Sprachkenntnisse gezielt ausbauen willst. Natürlich ist es auch als Klassenlektüre bestens geeignet.

Alle unsere Krimis werden von Muttersprachlern verfasst, so dass du sicher sein kannst, eine authentische Sprache kennenzulernen. Das Glossar zu diesem Buch wurde für phase6 vertont. Dort kannst du die Wörter zusätzlich trainieren.

Viel Spaß und Erfolg!

Inhalt

Danger Down Under

1 Ghosts and Memories

January, Summer in Merimubla, NSW, Australia

The sun is just coming up in Merimbula, <u>Australia</u> 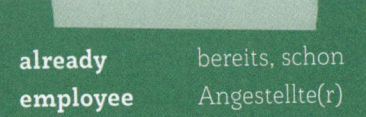.

already	bereits, schon
employee	Angestellte(r)

But Desmond "Des" Colby is **already** at his desk. Des is not alone. Matilda is with him. She is sitting on the floor at his feet.

They are in Des's office at Colby's Resort and Surfing School. Its guests and **employees** are all still asleep.

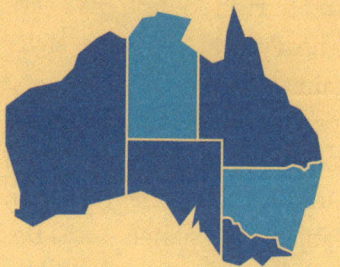

Welcome to Australia! Australien ist gleichzeitig die größte Insel und der kleinste Kontinent der Welt, auch als **Land Down Under** bekannt. Australien ist in sechs Bundesstaaten (= **states**) und zwei Territorien (= **territory**) unterteilt. New South Wales (NSW) ist am stärksten besiedelt.

Circa 450 km südöstlich von Sydney entfernt liegt das Surferparadies **Merimbula**.

But Des can't sleep. He doesn't have time for it. Des must write a letter – a very important letter. The problem is, Des hates writing. And this letter is very hard for him to write. It's not easy for Des to find the right words.

"How do I say it, Matilda?" Matilda **barks**. A short, loud bark. Des understands the Australian Shepherd.

He **sighs** and tells the dog, "OK, you're right. I should **just get on with it**!" So he does. Des writes for some minutes. Like always, writing makes his hand **hurt**. His head hurts, too. And his heart is heavy and sad. Des sighs again.

"It's not perfect, Matilda. Nothing is ever perfect. But I think it's OK," he tells her. Matilda **wags** her **tail**. Des **signs** his name to the letter. Then he puts down his pen.

"I just hope Stuart understands – and **forgives** me."

to bark	bellen
to sigh	seufzen
⚡ Just get on with it!	Mach einfach!
to hurt	wehtun
to wag (a tail)	wedeln (mit dem Schwanz)
to sign	unterschreiben
to forgive	vergeben

Exercise 1: Missing verbs.

Keep reading and fill in the gaps with the verbs in the right form.

| not open | can | stand up | be (2 x) | see | walk | stand |

Slowly, Des **1.** _Stand up_ – and so does Matilda. They **2.** _walk_ over to a big, glass door, but Des **3.** _Stand_ _not op_ it. He and Matilda just **4.** _See_ there, looking out at the Tasman Sea. To Des, the waves **seem** to **5.** _be_ dancing in the morning sun. **Suddenly**, he **6.** _be_ something on the water. "Look Matilda! There **7.** _is_ a ghost on the sea! **8.** _Can_ you see it, too?"

Beim Wortfeld **memory** (= Erinnerung) gibt es zwei Verben, die man leicht durcheinanderbringen kann:
to remember = sich an etw. Vergangenes erinnern;
to remind sb. of sth. = jdn. an etw. erinnern;
to remind sb. to do sth. = jdn. daran erinnern, etw. zu tun.
Beobachte beim Weiterlesen genau, wie die Wörter verwendet werden.

Matilda barks again, but it's a sad bark. Des can't really see a **ghost**. No, he is <u>remembering</u> 💡. Des is "seeing" himself. But in the memory, he's 16 years old again – not 67. And he's out on the sea, riding the waves on his surfboard. He can see Beth – his first and only love. In this memory,

to seem	erscheinen
suddenly	plötzlich
ghost	Gespenst, Geist
painful	schmerzhaft
to follow	folgen

Beth is only 15, and so beautiful. She's standing on the beach at Short Point with her surfboard. She's waving at him, and laughing. Des smiles at the memory. He and Beth <u>were</u> 💡 so young then – and so happy.

"What a great life!" he tells Matilda. But then, Des sighs again. "Or *mostly* great, Matilda. I just wish…"

He doesn't say what he wishes. Des is seeing other ghosts from his past. Not all of his memories are good ones. Some of them are very **painful**, too.

Matilda barks again. This time very loudly.

"You're right, Matilda. It's time for me to finish the job!"

Slowly, Des goes back to his desk and Matilda **follows** him.

was/were ist die einfache Vergangenheitsform (**simple past**) von **to be** (= sein). Es ist ein unregelmäßiges Verb und muss auswendig gelernt werden. **Been** ist das Partizip Perfekt. Das braucht man, um das **Present Perfect** (das Perfekt) zu bilden, z. B. *I have been at home all day.* = *Ich bin den ganzen Tag zu Hause gewesen.*

to explain	erklären
to expect	erwarten
to take care of sb.	sich um jmd. kümmern
finally	endlich
will	Testament
heirs *pl.*	Erben
condition	Bedingung
⚡ **to fire sb.**	jmd. feuern
to move (to)	*hier:* umziehen
special	besonders
to run sth.	etw. betreiben

"Not everyone <u>will</u> 💡 be happy about it," he **explains** to her. "Of course, Beth already knows. But Frank will be shocked. I **expect** Stuart will be angry. At first, he will hate the idea. But it will be good for him – and for Jeremy and Katie, too."

Matilda barks again. It seems she expects something.

"And of course it will be good for you, too, Matilda. Don't worry! Stuart's children will **take** great **care of you**!"

Matilda just looks at Stuart and he smiles. "Of course, Matilda! I know that you will be the one taking care of everybody. I'm going to miss you, girl."

Then Des sighs once more, and **finally**, he writes his new **will**.

Das Verb **will** (= werden) benutzt man, um über die Zukunft zu reden. Das Will-Future ist eine von vielen englischen Zukunftsformen und wird sehr oft verwendet. ACHTUNG! **Will** hat nichts mit dem deutschen Verb „**will**' – von **wollen** - zu tun! *I will go.* = *Ich* **werde** *gehen.* (NICHT *Ich* **will** *gehen!*) Die Kurzform von **will not** ist **won't**.

I am Desmond Colby. This is my LAST WILL and TESTAMENT. My **heirs** *are Stuart Styles of Bournemouth, England, and his children, Katherine (Katie) and Jeremy. But I have some* **conditions.** *These are:*

Exercise 2: Chronology.

Put the conditions of Des's will into the right order.

1	2	3	4	5	6	7
c	g	a	f	b	d	e

a) In that year, Stuart cannot **fire** anybody!

b) The two of them must also take good care of Matilda.

c) My heirs must **move to** Merimbula and live at Colby's.

d) She's a very **special** dog!

e) Finally, they should all try to be happy again.

f) And also, Katie and Jeremy must go to school here.

g) Then, Stuart must **run** Colby's Resort for at least one year!

Hier sind einige **häufig auftretende Wörter** in den **Übungsanweisungen**, die immer wieder vorkommen:

- unscramble = entschlüsseln
- missing = fehlend
- underline = unterstreichen
- match = zusammenpassen
- translate = übersetzen
- complete = vervollständigen
- gap = Lücke
- clues = Hinweise
- solution = Lösung
- Continue reading. = Lies weiter.
- Keep reading. = Lies weiter.
- Spot the mistakes. = Entdecke die Fehler.
- Fill in the gaps. = Füll die Lücken aus.
- Odd one out. = Ein Wort passt nicht in die Reihe.

Can you find Merimbula on the map of Australia?

2 Old and New History

April, Spring in Bournemouth *, Dorset, England*

⚡ **Damn you!**	Scher dich zum Teufel!
to shake	*hier:* zittern
to sip	nippen
lie	Lüge
cancer	Krebs (Krankheit)
unbelievable	unglaublich
tear	Träne
strange	komisch

"**Damn you**, Desmond Colby!" Stuart Styles says out loud. "How could you do this to me – and to Jeremy and Katie, too?" Stuart is very angry. He's holding some papers in his hands. He sees that his hands are **shaking** and sighs.

"I have to calm down," he says. "Katie and Jeremy will be home from school soon."

Stuart puts the papers down and picks up his cup of tea, which is cold now. He tries to think as he **sips** the cold tea. He can't. His head and heart are heavy and sad. They are full of too many memories, too many **lies** and too much history. It's sad and painful history, too.

Stuart leaves the table and goes to the kitchen window. From there, he can see out to the sea ☀. For a moment, he looks out at the waves on the English Channel. He can hear them, too. It is like they are singing. And the song is, "Des is dead." Somehow, Stuart just can't believe it. Des was not that old. But well, **cancer** does not care about how old somebody is.

The sea doesn't either, Stuart thinks bitterly.

He leaves the window and its view of the water. Then he goes back to the table. He reads Des's last will again. It is **unbelievable**!

"Damn you, Des!" he says again.

But Stuart has **tears** in his eyes.

That's **strange**, he thinks. He almost never cries anymore. Not since... No! He won't think about Ellen now. He can't. But Stuart's tears are falling faster. Some of them fall on a letter – a letter that Des wrote just weeks before he died.

Bournemouth (Aussprache /'bɔːrnməθ) liegt circa 172 km südwestlich von London am Ärmelkanal (= *the English Channel*) in Devon. Die Kleinstadt ist ein populärer Urlaubsort und bekannt für tolles Wetter, schöne Strände und gute Surfmöglichkeiten.

Achtung! **False friends**:
the sea = das Meer; der See = the lake.

Exercise 3: How much?

Keep reading and underline the right word(s) in Des's letter to Stuart!

...Stuart, I'm **1.** so / such sorry. I know you and the kids miss Ellen very **2.** much / a lot . She was **3.** so / such a wonderful person – and the **4.** good / best wife and mother. It is **5.** so / such tragic that she is dead. But her death was **6.** much / many months ago... it's more **7.** as / than a year now since the **accident**. Stuart, you and the kids must make **8.** some / any new memories! Please take the **inheritance**! Come to Merimbula! Come home! And Stuart, **tell** Katie and Jeremy **the truth**!"

"Hey Dad, we're home!" Stuart hears his daughter Katie say. She's coming into the kitchen with Jeremy, his son.
"Dad! What's wrong?" Jeremy **cries out**. "Are you sick?"
"Why are you crying, Dad?" Katie asks. "Is there bad news?"

accident	Unfall
inheritance	Erbe
to tell the truth	die Wahrheit sagen
to cry out	aufschreien
voice	Stimme
worried	besorgt
overweight	übergewichtig
to notice	(be-)merken
unhealthy	ungesund
though	*hier:* aber, jedoch
delicious	lecker
recipe	(Koch)rezept

"Is it another death, Dad?" Jeremy asks. His **voice** is shaking.

At first, Stuart can't speak. He just shakes his head and looks at his two teenage children.

They seem so sad, he thinks – and **worried**, too. Almost depressed. 16-year-old Katie is so thin. Too thin! And Jeremy! My God, he'll be 15 in a few months! He's getting so tall. Like me – and like Ellen. But Jeremy is also **overweight**, Stuart **notices**. His son looks **unhealthy**. So does Katie. Maybe... maybe Des was right...?

"Dad! Talk to us!" Jeremy cries out – almost shouting now.

"Jeremy! Calm down. I'm OK. Don't worry. It's just..."

"Just what, Dad?" Katie says.

"Just this," Stuart says. He picks up the will and gives it to Katie to read. He won't show the kids the letter from Des, **though**. Not yet – maybe not ever.

"But Dad, who is – or who was – Desmond Colby?" Katie asks. It's dinnertime, and the family are sitting together at the kitchen table. They are eating chicken soup.

It's **delicious**, Jeremy thinks. It tastes almost like Mum's. His dad uses her **recipe**. But Mum always...

Jeremy suddenly puts down his spoon. He's not hungry anymore – at least not for soup.

to interrupt	unterbrechen
grave	Grab
whole	ganz
to jump up	aufspringen
to slam	zuknallen

"I don't want to move to Australia!" he says loudly. "Do we have to do it, Dad?"

"Well, no, we don't have to, Jeremy. But maybe we should think about it. It could be just what we all need. And it..."

"I don't need to think about it!" Jeremy **interrupts**. "I don't know anybody there. My friends and school are here in Bournemouth! And this is where Mum's **grave** is." Jeremy stops talking. He's got tears in his eyes.

Katie doesn't see them. She's looking at her dad and smiling.

"Well, I think it's a great idea, Dad! Australia! So cool! There are koala bears 💡 and kangaroos, and great surfing! But what I don't understand is, why are we this Desmond person's heirs? How do you – I mean, how did you know him?"

"Ah Katie, it's a long story. Des is – or he was – one of my Dad's best friends. But Des was younger than my dad, and younger than my mother, too."

Australien hat circa eine Million einheimische Pflanzen- und Tierarten. Die **Koalabären** und Kängurus gehören zu den bekanntesten australischen Tieren. Wusstest du, dass der Koalabär gar kein Bär ist, sondern wie das Känguru ein Beuteltier (= **marsupial**)?

Exercise 4: The past.

Keep reading about Stuart's old family history. Put the missing verbs in the simple past!

"Oh!" Katie says. "I **1.** not know _____ that Grandpa

Mark **2.** have _____ a friend in Australia!"

"Um, yes. They **3.** know _____ each other from

surfing holidays. When I **4.** be _____ a child, my

family **5.** visit _____ Merimbula a lot. **Actually** ,

that is where I first **6.** learn _____ to surf. Des and

my parents **7.** be _____ my first teachers."

That's all true, Stuart thinks. Just not the **whole** truth.
"Well, I'm never going surfing again!" Jeremy suddenly shouts.
"And I am *not* moving to Australia!"
Then he **jumps up** from the table and runs to his room.
"Jeremy! Come back this minute!" Stuart says loudly. They
hear Jeremy's bedroom door **slam**. Stuart starts to follow him.

Achtung! **False friends**:
actually = wirklich, tatsächlich; aktuell = currently.

to leave sb. alone	jmd. in Ruhe lassen
exciting	aufregend
fault	Schuld
to be to blame	an etw. Schuld sein
to whisper	flüstern
to save	retten
to start over	neu anfangen

"Don't, Dad. Just **leave him alone** for a bit." Katie says. "Some time alone always calms him down." She doesn't tell her dad that Jeremy has a new way of calming down: he eats sweets. Lots of them.

"Yes, I know. But Jeremy hates it when things change. He's like me. I like things to stay the same."

"Well, I like changes, Dad – at least, nice ones!" Katie says. "Changes can be fun – and **exciting**. But Jeremy's big problem isn't change, Dad. Jeremy hates himself."

"What?" Stuart says. "How can you say that, Katie?"

"Because it's the truth! Jeremy thinks it's his **fault** that Mum died. Don't you know that? And you know what? He's right! It *is* his fault. But **I'm to blame**, too. And so are you!"

Suddenly, Katie jumps up and runs to her room, too. Stuart hears another door slam. And then he hears Katie crying.

Katie is right – but she is also wrong. Katie and Jeremy are *not* to blame for Ellen's death.

"It's my fault," Stuart **whispers**. "I'm the one who couldn't... didn't **save** her." He feels like crying again, but he doesn't have any tears left. Stuart just sits sadly at the kitchen table with the cold chicken soup – and his memories. He remembers Ellen – her life, their love, and how she died. It feels like she is there and whispering to him: "Stuart, save our children!" Then it is Des he hears – or the ghost of Des – whispering again and again: "Come to Merimbula, Stuart. Come home and **start over**."

Exercise 5: Matching.

Match the pictures to the words!

1. ☐ thin

a)

2. ☐ overweight

b)

3. ☐ delicious

c)

4. ☐ whisper

d)

5. ☐ jump

e)

Wales

West Midlands

Bristol Channel

Gloucestershire

South
Gloucestershire

Swindon

Bristol

North
Somerset

Bath and
North East
Somerset

Wiltshire

Sou
Eas

Somerset

Devon

Dorset

Poole

Bournemouth

Cornwall

Torbay

Plymouth

English Channel

N
W E
S

3 Starting Over Down Under

7:00 a.m., October, spring 💡 *in Merimubla, AUS*

The sun is just coming up in Merimbula. Katie is in her new bedroom in Des's old house at Colby's Resort. It's only a month since they moved here from Bournemouth. But Katy already loves living here. And her new room is fabulous! Katie already has her favourite posters on the walls, and her favou-

Die vier Jahreszeiten (= **the four seasons**) sind in Australien genau umgekehrt: Der Frühling dauert in Australien von September bis November und Weihnachten ist im Sommer (Dezember bis Februar).

rite photo of her mum is on Katie's desk. It is in front of a **huge** window. Katie is sitting at the desk right now. She is writing in her **journal** – or trying to write. **Instead**, she keeps looking out of the window at the beach and the Tasman Sea. Katie loves watching the sun rising over the sea.

huge	riesig
journal	Tagebuch
instead	stattdessen
facilities manager	Hausmeister
⚡ **Oh well...**	Tja ...
⚡ **That's his business!**	Das geht mich nichts an!
opposite	gegenüber

But this morning, Katie is also watching Frank Morris. He's Des Colby's nephew and the **facilities manager** at Colby's Resort.

He seems nice enough, Katie thinks. But what's he doing so early in the morning? Normally, he doesn't start work until 8:00.

Oh well, **that's his business**, Katie thinks and closes her journal.

In Australien, wie auch in Großbritannien, müssen fast alle Schüler*innen Schuluniform tragen. Normalerweise heißt das für Jungen eine lange oder kurze Hose (= **trousers/shorts**), für Mädchen Hose oder Rock (= **skirt**), dazu ein Polohemd oder Hemd (= **shirt**), oft mit Krawatte (= **tie**), Pulli (= **jumper**) und Blazer dazu. Die Regeln für Schuluniformen sind an vielen Schulen sehr streng!

Opposite the huge window, there is a big oval mirror. Katie goes to it now. She wants to see how she looks in her new school uniform 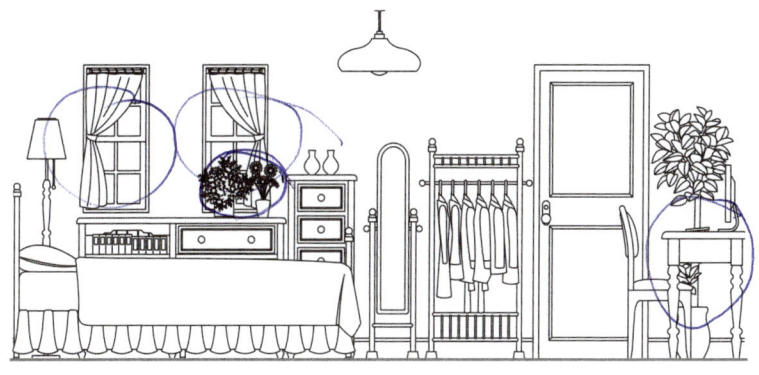. It's nicer than the one she had in England.

Exercise 6: Katie's Room?

Fill in the gaps to say what is wrong with the picture of Katie's new room!

1. There are two small windows ~~one not one~~ *instead* of one huge one.

2. The desk is not in ___*the Front*___ of the window.

3. The mirror is not ~~in other~~ *Opposite* the bed.

4. There are not any posters on the _____.

5. The desk does not have a *Picture now* on it.

⚡ **right on cue**	wie gerufen
part-time	Teilzeit
in fact	und zwar
gorgeous	sehr attraktiv
sweetheart	Süße(r), Schatz

"The uniform actually looks good on me," Katie whispers to herself. "I hope Mike thinks so, too!"

Right on cue, her phone starts playing a ringtone. It's the special one she already has for Mike Amis.

"G'day 💡, Mike!" Katie says. There is a smile in her voice.

"G'day, Katie!" Mike answers and he laughs. "You're already using Australian slang. Good on ya, mate!"

"Thanks! I mean ta!" Katie says. "A nice surfer is helping me." Katie laughs. Mike *is* that nice surfer. He works **part-time** at Colby's at the surf school. He is also very good-looking. **In fact**, Katie thinks, he's **gorgeous** – and a real **sweetheart**, too!

Talk like an Australian! Wie jedes Land hat Australien seinen eigenen **Slang**. Hier eine kleine Auswahl:

G'day = hello,
avro = afternoon,
heaps = lots,
barbie = barbeque,
fair dinkum = real, true.

Ebenso wird man überall mit **mate** (= Kumpel) angesprochen! Die Australier lieben es auch, Wörter zu kürzen, z. B. **defo** = definitely, **postie** = postman/woman und **brekky** = breakfast.

"A nice surfer, huh? Lucky you!" Mike says, laughing. "Listen, Grace and I will come by to get you and Jeremy. We can walk to the bus stop together."

⚡ **What on earth...?!** Was zum Teufel ...?!

to look sth. up nachschlagen

"Great! Ta!" says Katie, laughing again.

"And also, some of us want to go surfing after school. We're going to Short Point Beach. Do you want to come, too?"

"Oh yes – defo! I'm really looking forward to 💡 trying out the waves there! But I have to ask my dad first. I'll tell you later, OK?"

"Sure, no wuckers!"

"**What on earth** does 'no wuckers' mean?" Katie asks. "Is it something like 'no problem'?"

"Exactly! Hey Katie, you're great at Australian dialect!" Mike says. "Maybe I'll teach you the word 'pash' next. No, don't ask what it means. I'll show you! Cheerio!"

"Cheerio!" says Katie.

She likes learning Australian slang with Mike. She'd like to learn some other things from him, too. But what is this 'pash?' Katie quickly **looks it up** online.

Phrasal Verbs bestehen aus einem Verb plus Partikel (Adverb/Präposition). Die Bedeutung des Verbs ändert sich, je nachdem welcher Partikel verwendet wird, z. B.:
to look after – sich kümmern; **to look for** – suchen; **to look at** – ansehen; **to look through** – durchblättern; **to look forward to** – sich auf etwas freuen; **to look sth. up** – nachschlagen.

"Oh wow!" she says and **giggles**. "Pash" means "kissing!"
Katie looks in the mirror again. Her eyes are **sparkling** and she looks very excited. Katie whispers to herself.
"Keep cool Katie! And go slow. No 'pashing' before you know Mike better!" Katie giggles again. I sound like Mum, she thinks. Then Katie sighs. She still misses her mum. She even talks to her sometimes. "Mum? You'd really like Mike. And..."
Katie suddenly hears screaming. It's coming from Jeremy's room right next door!

Exercise 7: Fill in the gaps.

Fill in the words in the right gap!

sweetheart   earth   journal   shore   sparkling

part-time

1. What on _earth_ is happening?

2. She's sitting on the _shose_.

3. He's a _sweetheght_.

4. I'm writing in my _journal_.

5. He works _part-time_.

6. It's shiny and _sparling_.

Jeremy is dreaming. He can hear the waves and sees himself riding them on his surfboard. He's 13. Dad and Katie are on the **shore**. They are waving at him. Mum is on the water with Jeremy. She's so great, Jeremy thinks. Mum surfs even better than Dad! Jeremy waves at her and calls out, "Hey Mum!

to giggle	kichern
sparkling	glitzernd
shore	Ufer, Küste
⚡ Watch out!	Pass auf!
to scream	schreien
to whine	winseln
lick	lecken
to hug	umarmen
just beyond	direkt dahinter

Look at me!" Then Jeremy does a handstand on his board. He waves at his mum with his feet!

His mum watches him, laughing. And for a moment, Ellen Styles stops concentrating on the sea. Suddenly, she's screaming, "Jeremy! **Watch out**! Behind you!" Then she is falling. And now Jeremy is **screaming**, "Mum! Mum! Watch out!" And then he is falling too...

Matilda is **whining** next to Jeremy's bed, and he wakes up. He opens his eyes and Matilda **licks** his face. Jeremy puts his arms around the dog. He **hugs** her and whispers, "Oh Matilda! I'm so glad you're here!"

Matilda barks, and then she jumps off the bed. She runs over to a pair of glass doors. They open out onto a little terrace and a small garden. **Just beyond** that is the sea.

Jeremy gets out of bed and walks to the doors.

"What's up, Matilda? Do you want to go outside? Or can you see something?" Jeremy looks out of the glass doors. He's surprised at what he sees. It's Frank. He has a pair of **binoculars** around his neck and is holding his phone.

"Jeremy? Are you OK?" Katie asks as she opens the door to her brother's new room. She sees Jeremy standing outside on the terrace. He is in his pyjamas.

"I heard you screaming and Matilda whining. Was it... was it the **nightmare**?"

Exercise 8: Useful adverbs.

Keep reading and put the adverbs in the right gap!

again   else   too   inside   already   just   so   since

"Yeah," Jeremy says and comes **1.** _inside_ . "It's the

first time **2.** _since_ we moved here. I thought..."

"What?" Katie asks, but she **3.** _again_ knows.

"That I wouldn't have the nightmare **4.** _already_ ."

"Yeah, I hoped that, **5.** _too_ . But look, Jeremy. We moved

to Australia **6.** _so_ four weeks ago. **7.** _else_

really, it is getting better, isn't it? And do you know something

8. _just_ ? You seem to be feeling better, too. The Land

Down Under 💡 isn't so bad, is it?"

"No, it isn't. I do actually like it here. And I *am* better! But…"

"But what?" Katie asks Jeremy. Jeremy doesn't know how to explain to Katie. He has a "feeling" that something strange is going on at Colby's, but he just isn't sure what it is. It has something to do with Des Colby's nephew,

binoculars *pl.*	Fernglas
nightmare	Alptraum
to get in trouble	Ärger kriegen
to change the subject	das Thema wechseln

Frank. But what? The facilities manager always seems very friendly. And Jeremy doesn't want Frank **to get into trouble**. So he says to Katie, "But please don't tell Dad about the nightmare, OK? He'll worry."

Then, Jeremy decides to **change the subject**.

"What time is it?"

Warum wird Australien oft umgangssprachlich das Land **Down Under** genannt? Der Spitzname „Down Under" entstand aufgrund der europäischen Entdecker, die ein Land unterhalb des asiatischen Kontinents suchten und Australien liegt „unter" dem Äquator. Allerdings benutzen die Australier selbst diesen Namen selten!

"It's 7:15! It's time for you to get ready for school! Then come to the kitchen. Dad is making us a special fry-up 💡 for our first day of school. Oh! And Mike and Grace are going to walk with us to the bus stop. So hurry up!"

"Cool!" Jeremy says and smiles at Katie.

Katie smiles back at her little brother and leaves his room. She closes the door **gently** behind her. Then she sighs. Should she tell Dad about Jeremy's nightmare? But no, Jeremy is right. Dad will worry.

gently	sanft
to tip sb. off	jmd. warnen

And then, Katie thinks, he won't let me go to Short Point. He'll make me babysit Jeremy, instead. Anyway, Jeremy is OK now. This new start here Down Under is good for him. For all of us!

Jeremy hugs Matilda again.

"Thanks for **tipping me off** about Frank. You can help me

Ein **fry-up** – anders bekannt als **English breakfast** – ist ein beliebtes üppiges Frühstück in Australien und Großbritannien (**to fry** = braten). Hier wird tatsächlich ALLES gebraten: **fried eggs** (= Spiegeleier), **bacon** (= Speck), **sausages** (= Würstchen), **tomato**, **mushrooms** (= Champignons) und **baked beans** (= Bohnen in Tomatensoße). Nicht wirklich gesund – aber lecker! Und macht auf jeden Fall satt!

watch him!" Jeremy puts on his school uniform. It fits him well. Jeremy is already **losing some weight**. He even goes swimming in the sea – though only if Matilda goes with him. He is already making new friends, too.

to lose weight	(Gewicht) abnehmen
⚡ **have a crush on sb.**	in jdn. verknallt sein
to scratch	kratzen
to continue	*hier:* weiterreden
⚡ **show sb. the ropes**	jdn. mit allem vertraut machen
to frown	die Stirn runzeln

He tells Matilda, "I really like Mike! I think Katie **has a crush on** him. Mike seems to have one on her, too!"

Matilda barks once and Jeremy **scratches** her gently behind her ears. Matilda likes that and wags her tail.

"Mike's sister, Grace, is lots of fun," Jeremy **continues**. "And she's really nice, too. Grace says she'll **show me the ropes** at the new school in Bega 💡."

Jeremy stops talking and **frowns**. There isn't a high school in Merimbula. That's why the older kids here have to go to high school somewhere else. In Bournemouth, Jeremy could just walk or ride his bike to school.

"A lot of things here in Australia are very different," he tells

Obwohl die Kleinstadt **Bega** in Australien nur knapp über 4.100 Einwohner hat, besuchen an die 1.000 Jugendliche die dortige *high school*. Der Grund? Bega hat ein sehr großes ländliches Einzugsgebiet: das **Bega Valley Shire**.

weird	seltsam
to sneak around	(herum)schleichen
sure	sicher
secretly	heimlich
crunchy	knusprig
to sulk	schmollen

Matilda. "And some things are just **weird**." Jeremy is thinking about Frank again.

"Do you notice the way Frank looks at me sometimes, Matilda? And at Katie and Grace, too. And he's always **sneaking around**." Jeremy shakes his head. "Anyway, I have to hurry now. It's a bad idea to be late on the first day!"

Matilda barks once, but then she whines again.
"Ah, don't worry, Matilda. I'm **sure** it will all be fine."
Matilda doesn't bark. She doesn't wag her tail, either.

Exercise 9: Pronouns.

Keep reading and underline the correct pronoun!

But after Jeremy is dressed, **1.** ~~he~~ / she follows **2.** his / ~~him~~

to the big kitchen where **3.** she / ~~her~~ new family eats

4. they / ~~their~~ fry-up. Jeremy **secretly** gives Matilda

5. ~~his~~ / him two pieces of bacon. The dog loves the taste of

6. them / ~~they~~ – so salty and **crunchy**! Katie asks if she

can go to Short Point later, but **7.** ~~her~~ / she Dad says no.

8. "Oh Dad! Please let me / ~~my~~ go!" But **9.** ~~he~~ / him says no

again, and Katie **sulks**.

After breakfast, the kids leave the house.
Matilda follows them. So does their dad, who
reminds Matilda of Des.
She whines a little, and Jeremy tells her,
"Don't be sad, Matilda. I'll be back... back
home soon!"

4 Unfair and Mean

8:00 am, Merimbula

In front of the house at Colby's Resort, Stuart says, "Cheerio, Katie! Have a great first day!"

But Katie does not say "cheerio" to her dad. She is still **mad at him** and sulking.

to be mad at sb.	auf jmd. wütend sein
mean	gemein, fies
experienced	erfahren

It's so unfair! she thinks. Sometimes, Dad is so **mean** to me! Why can't I go with Mike and his friends to Short Point? Why do I have to stay home? Oh right, because of Jeremy. It's just not fair!

"And Jeremy," Stuart continues. "You have a good day, too. Katie will help you with your homework after school, son. Right, Katie?" Stuart does not wait for her to answer. He knows Katie is mad at him. But Short Point can be a very dangerous

Die Surfer-Welt hat teilweise eine eigene Sprache, z. B. **to wipe out** = von einem Surfbrett stürzen; **surf's up** = die Wellen sind bestens fürs Surfen; **gnarly waves** sind Wellen, die besonders aufregend UND gefährlich sind. Ein **agro** ist ein aggressiver, unhöflicher Surfer, während **dude/dudette** ein freundlicher Name für Surfer/Surferin ist.

place, with <u>gnarly</u>  waves even in spring. It's true that Katie is already an excellent surfer, Stuart tells himself. She learned it from Ellen – and from me. It's just Katie is so young. She's not **experienced**. Not like Ellen. But Ellen's experience didn't save her when she wiped out... No. Stuart wants to take Katie to Short Point himself – but later.

In summer, when the surf's up. Like in the past... like it was that time he saw Des at Short Point – out on the water surfing. Surfing with Beth.

"Dad! Are you listening to me?" Jeremy asks.

solution — Lösung
⚡ **to hang out with** — mit jmd. rumhängen

What on earth is wrong with Dad? Jeremy thinks. It looks as if Dad has seen a ghost!

Jeremy tries again.

"Dad! I said maybe there won't be any homework today. And even if there is, Katie doesn't have to help me!" Jeremy smiles at his dad and then at Katie. It's a great **solution**! Now, maybe Katie can go surfing with Mike. And maybe... maybe I will even make a new friend at school today. Someone like me. Somebody to just **hang out with**.

And then Jeremy sees Mike. He's walking up to Katie.

Grace is behind him – but she is not alone.

She's whispering to another girl. A very pretty girl, too. Jeremy doesn't know her. He thinks he hears Grace say his name. The other girl laughs. But it's not a nice laugh. Who is she?

"Have you met 💡 Keira?" Grace asks Jeremy. They are walking to the bus stop now. "Keira is our age, and she's in our year at school, too."

"No, we haven't met yet," Jeremy says. He looks at the other girl. He smiles and says, "Hi, Keira, I'm Jeremy!"

"Yeah, I know who you are," Keira says. Her voice is cold and

Have you met...? (= Hast du ... schon kennengelernt?) ist ein Beispiel für das **Present Perfect**: Es wird aus dem Hilfsverb **have/has** plus der 3. Form des Verbs (hier: **met** von **to meet**) zusammengesetzt.

unfriendly. "Your dad's the new **owner** of Colby's, right?" Keira continues. "And you and your sister are Mr Desmond's heirs, too. So I guess you're the new rich kids in town, right?"

owner	Besitzer
rudely	unhöflich
glad	froh
except	außer
polite	höflich

"Um, I... well, my dad *is* running Colby's now," Jeremy says.

"And Katie and I are new here. But I don't think we are..."

"Oh, whatever ," Keira interrupts him **rudely**. I don't really care about *you*. I want to know about your father. He's my grandma's new boss!"

"Oh!" Jeremy says. He's surprised. But that explains why this Keira knows so much about him and his family.

"What's your grandma's name?" Jeremy asks quickly. He's **glad** to change the subject! "I think I've met everybody who works at Colby's – except for the manager. So far, everybody seems really nice." Jeremy almost says, "**except** you". But he is still trying to be **polite** – not rude, like Keira.

Whatever hat viele verschiedene Bedeutungen, es kommt ganz auf den Kontext an. Hier meint Keira so etwas wie „meinetwegen" oder „(ist mir) egal." Andere Beispiele:

Whatever you do = Was du auch tust.
Whatever you want = Was immer du willst.
Whatever happens = Egal, was passiert.

"My granny *is* the manager of Colby's. Her name is Beth. Beth Jackson," Keira tells him slowly. Keira is looking at Jeremy's face very **closely**. This makes him nervous. And when Jeremy is nervous, sometimes he doesn't talk at all – but other times, he talks too much. Like now.

Exercise 10: Present perfect.

Keep reading and put either *have* or *has* into the gap to form the present perfect!

"Really? I **1.** _have_ heard lots of great things about your grandma! She **2.** _has_ been the manager at Colby's for a long time, right? My dad **3.** _has_ told me a little about her. But I **4.** _have_ not met her yet. She's on holiday, right? Frank says she **5.** _has_ gone to Sydney. I **6.** _have_ been there once – but only at the airport when..."

Jeremy suddenly stops talking.
Keira is staring at him like he is some kind of **weirdo**.
"My Granny Beth and I have *both* been on holiday! But not in Sydney!" Keira says, slowly and loudly.
It's like she thinks I'm stupid, Jeremy thinks.
"But now we're back home," she adds. "And I only want to know one thing. Is your dad going to fire my Granny Beth?"
"What?" Jeremy asks.

"It's an easy question, *English-boy*," Keira says. "You Pommies ! You're all the same!"

"Keira!" Grace finally says something, too. "Stop being so mean to Jeremy! What's wrong with you?"

"It's... it's OK, Grace," Jeremy says slowly. He's glad Grace is finally **sticking up for him**. But he can stick up for himself.

"Well, I *am* English, Keira. I just don't understand why that's a problem for you. I don't even know what a ‚Pommy' is. I guess it isn't good. Do you want to tell me?"

Keira starts to feel **ashamed**. She knows she has been very rude. It's just...

"**Never mind**!" Jeremy tells Keira when she doesn't say anything. "I can look it up. But Keira, your grandma doesn't have to worry. My dad isn't going to fire her. I mean, why would he do that? Everybody says that Beth, I mean Mrs Jackson, is just the best!"

"She is!" Keira says. And then she **realizes**: Jeremy *doesn't know*! And I can't tell him! At least I shouldn't tell him. But...

closely	genau, nah
⚡ **weirdo**	Spinner
⚡ **to stick up for sb.**	für jmd. eintreten
ashamed	beschämt
⚡ **Never mind!**	Macht nix! Was soll's!
to realize	wahrnehmen

Ein **Pommy** (oder **Pom**) ist ein abwertendes Wort, welches die Australier und Neuseeländer für Engländer benutzen.

Suddenly, Jeremy hears his sister calling out: "Jeremy! Grace! Keira!" She and Mike are already at the bus stop.
"Come on! Hurry up!" Mike shouts. "The bus is coming!"
Jeremy sees it. And he sees Mike holding Katie's hand!

Exercise II: How people behave.

Identify how the boy is behaving in the pictures, then fill in the gaps with the adjective!

unfriendly   ashamed   furious   nervous

1. *unfrendly*

2. *norvous*

3. *favios*

4. *as hamod*

5 Dangerous Kangaroos

8:20 a.m., the Princes Highway, 15 km from Bega

The school bus is traveling fast along the A1 <u>Princes Highway</u> 💡 towards Bega. The landscape along the highway is beautiful. "Oh Mike, look! There's a kangaroo!" Katie says. "It's so sweet! Oh! And there's another one!" She laughs and Mike smiles at her.

"We just call them 'roos' here, Katie," Mike says. "And well, they are kind of sweet, but they can be dangerous, too." Mike thinks Katie is very sweet – and so pretty! She's looking at Mike now and her eyes are sparkling. Mike is wondering:

Der **Princes Highway** ist eine 1.941 km lange Hauptverkehrsader zwischen Sydney und Adelaide, die sich meistens an der Küste entlang schlängelt und traumhafte Ausblicke bietet. Sie führt durch die drei Bundesstaaten New South Wales, Victoria und South Australia. Das „fehlende" Apostroph bei Princes (eigentlich = Prince's) ist eine Besonderheit.

cheek	Wange
upset	verärgert
cruel	grausam
to reach	erreichen

Could I show Katie what pash means right now? Can I risk it?

He's sitting with Katie at the back of the bus. Grace and Keira are near the front. The two girls are whispering together.

Good, Mike thinks. They can't see me. And there is Katie's little brother. He has a seat alone in the middle of the bus. Mike sees Jeremy just staring out the window. He won't notice me, Mike thinks. I can give Katie a quick kiss on the **cheek**. But now, Katie is looking at her little brother, too.

"Jeremy looks a little lost, Mike," she says. "And a little **upset** as well. Maybe I should go and sit with him for a bit."

Jeremy *is* upset. In fact, he is more than upset. Jeremy is mad. Mad at Keira.

Aboriginal Australian peoples sind die Ureinwohner Australiens (Die verbreitete Sammelbezeichnung Aborigines sollte man heutzutage nicht mehr benutzen.). Sie besiedelten den Kontinent vor etwa 40.000 – 60.000 Jahren. 1788 fing die Kolonisation Australiens durch die Briten an – mit verheerenden Konsequenzen für die Ureinwohner. Eingeschleppte Krankheiten, gewaltsame Auseinandersetzungen und tödlichen Massaker sind nur einige Beispiele der negativen Auswirkungen.

Why was she so mean to me? he wonders. It's not fair! I haven't done anything to her! I don't even know her! What's up with her? Is she a racist? Jeremy doesn't think so. Keira's skin is just a little darker than Dad's is, and mine, too. So it's not racism. Maybe Keira just doesn't like English people. But it isn't my fault that English people were so horrible and **cruel** to Australia's Aboriginal peoples 💡.

I wish I could talk to Mum about this, Jeremy thinks. She always gives... gave me great advice.

Then he sighs. He can't talk to his mum. But he knows what she would say: Just talk to Keira. Just ask her. And then listen to what she says.

Jeremy decides to risk it.

Exercise 12: Adjective or adverb?

Keep reading and underline the right word!

He stands up **1.** quick / quickly , but he has to walk

2. slow / slowly to the girls. The bus is still going very

3. fast / fastly . It is not **4.** easy / easily for Jeremy to walk

5. careful / carefully . Jeremy **reaches** the girls' seat just as

the bus comes to a **6.** dangerous / dangerously curve.

Suddenly, he hears an **7.** extremely / extreme loud shout:

"Damn roos!" It's the driver.

Then, everything seems to be happening in **8.** slow / slowly

motion. It's a **9.** strange / strangely feeling.

| to steer | lenken |
| truck | Lastwagen |

Jeremy sees kangaroos jumping on the highway – right in front of the bus. The driver tries to slow the bus down and **steer** it away from the roos. Jeremy hears Katie scream:

"Jeremy! Watch Out! Sit back down!"

A big **truck** comes into the curve from the other direction. It's travelling fast – and coming right at them! Jeremy hears a crash. And then he is flying through the air. For what feels like a long time, Jeremy does not hear anything – except for Katie screaming at him and the ghosts in his dreams.

6 Nightmare

8:25 a.m., Colby's Resort, Merimbula
Matilda is whining. She has been nervous all morning. She **senses** that something is wrong. It's trouble – big trouble! Danger is in the air! Somehow, Matilda knows: it's bad. But the people at Colby's don't know it. Not yet.

"What on earth is wrong with that dog?" Frank Morris asks Stuart.
"She never made such horrible noises when Des was alive!" Frank **complains**.
Frank sounds like he is whining, too, Stuart thinks. But Frank was always a whiner. Stuart and Frank are in Des's old office. It's now Stuart's office.

It's **bizarre**, thinks Stuart. It's like I am in a movie about time travel – or **reincarnation**! As if I have suddenly become Des! Stuart shakes his head. It definitely feels weird!
Nevertheless, Stuart

to sense	spüren, ahnen
to complain	sich beschweren
bizarre	seltsam, wunderlich
reincarnation	Wiedergeburt
nevertheless	nichtsdestotrotz
to punch	schlagen
stretcher	Trage, Bahre

likes his new job and the new life in Australia. OK, so he hasn't seen Beth yet... He is meeting her after lunch. He knows it will be strange – painful, even. For both of them. Though who knows? Perhaps it will be OK...

Right now, Stuart has another problem. In fact, it is his only complaint about being back Down Under. The problem has a name: Frank Morris. Stuart doesn't like Frank. And Frank does not like him, either. Things have happened in the past... Stuart looks at Frank now. He reminds himself: Keep calm. Be professional. Don't **punch** Frank. And don't shout.

8:45 a.m., Princes Highway, near Bega

Katie hears lots of people shouting. She hears "Get the rest of the kids out of the bus!" or "Call for more ambulances!" and "We need a **stretcher** here. Now!" And then, there is a softer voice. It is saying, "Sweetheart, let me help you." It's a gentle voice, a woman's voice.

Mum? Katie whispers – but only inside her head. God, it hurts! Katie's eyes are closed. She's afraid to open them and see the reality.

This can't be real. It's a bad dream, Katie tells herself. It's a nightmare.

Achtung! **False friends**: **to become** = werden; bekommen = **to get** oder **to receive sth**. Wenn Stuart denkt: *As if I have suddenly become Des*, meint er: *Als wäre ich plötzlich Des geworden*. Aber: *Er bekam ein neues Surfbrett.* = He got/received a new surfboard.

8:45 a.m., Colby's Resort, Merimbula

Now Matilda is barking **frantically**. Her "people" hear her, but they are not **getting the message**. They are too **busy**. Busy with their little human lives.

"I don't know what's wrong with Matilda," Stuart says. "I guess 💡 she just misses Jeremy and Katie."

"Maybe. But *I* think the dog is still missing Des," Frank says. "Like we all do – except for you, Stuart. You weren't here the last twenty years or so. Des changed a lot after..."

"I'm sure he did change. We all have," Stuart tells Frank.

But Frank hasn't changed, he thinks. He's still a horrible person. And **recently** he has heard bad things about Frank. No surprises there! But are they true? Stuart wonders.

He realizes he's getting angry. Time to get back to business.

Das Wort **guess** hat unterschiedliche Bedeutungen: Wörtlich übersetzt, heißt es (er)raten, aber in der Umgangssprache kann es auch bedeuten: denken, annehmen, vermuten (wie hier im Text: *I guess she just misses...* Ich glaube, sie vermisst ...). Ebenso kann *guess* als Zustimmung benutzt werden, z. B. *I don't think she is coming now. – I guess so.* (= Ja, du hast wahrscheinlich recht.)

"We can talk about the past some other time, Frank. The reason I asked you to come to my office is that some guests are complaining. They say they have the feeling that somebody is watching them. Two **female** guests say someone keeps sneaking around outside their bungalows. And finally, some guests are missing things – things like **wallets,** electronic **devices,** and some **jewellery**. So, it looks as if someone at Colby's is stealing things. Do you know anything about it Frank?"

frantically	hektisch
⚡ **to get the message**	kapieren
busy	beschäftigt
recently	in letzter Zeit
female	weiblich
wallet	Brieftasche
devices	Geräte
jewellery	Schmuck
eavesdropping	lauschen

Beth Jackson is worrying. She is standing outside the door of Des's... Stuart's office. Beth has got her ear to the door. She is listening to Frank and Stuart... to *Mr Styles*, her new boss. Beth knows that **eavesdropping** is wrong. But she *has* to know what is happening at Colby's. Beth is very worried about the resort, about Frank, and about Stuart. Oh God! What will it be like to see him again? How can she work with him? And Beth is really worried about her grand-daughter. Keira is...

Suddenly, Beth's phone vibrates. There's a new message. She'll read it later. Beth wants answers. So she keeps listening – and worrying.

dear	Schatz, Liebling
oxygen	Sauerstoff
to breathe	atmen
sticky	klebrig
CPR (Cardio pulmonary Resuscitation)	Herz-Lungen-Wiederbelebung, Reanimation
Keep fighting!	Kämpf weiter!
to pour	fließen
to bury	begraben
to comfort	trösten

8:50 a.m., Princes Highway, near Bega

The nice rescue worker is still talking.

"Sweetie, can you hear me? Can you talk to me, **dear**?"

Katie cannot. She is in shock. She is sitting on some grass next to the Princes Highway. She is watching two other rescue workers carrying Mike out of the bus on a stretcher.

"Is he… is Mike… is he still alive?" she finally whispers.

"Yes, dear," the rescue worker says. "See? He has an **oxygen** mask on. Now, can you tell me your name?"

Katie just shakes her head. Oxygen. Air. Something about trying to get Jeremy to **breathe**. No, don't think about it, a voice in Katie's head whispers. She sees Grace. Two rescuers are helping Mike's sister into an ambulance.

Slowly, Katie puts a hand on her head. It's **sticky**. She takes her hand away and looks at it. It's covered in blood. And so is her new school uniform.

Is that my blood? She tries to remember. Or is it Mike's – or Jeremy's? I know I gave him **CPR** in the bus. But did it work? Did he **keep fighting**? Katie whispers his name, "Jeremy…"

"What dear?" the rescuer asks. And then Katie is crying. The tears are **pouring** down her face. Katie **buries** her head in her hands. The rescuer puts an arm around Katie to **comfort** her.

"Shush, sweetie," she says. "Everything will be OK."

Exercise 13: Fill in the gaps.

What is going on in the pictures? Fill in the gaps with words you have just learned!

The **1.** r _est_ _ _ w _olkers_ are taking the

boy on a **2.** s _troller_ _ _ over to a waiting

3. a _mbulance_ .

Most of the people here are busy with their

4. e _lectronic_ d _iwoise_ , but the

man on the left is trying to steal someone's

5. w _allet_ .

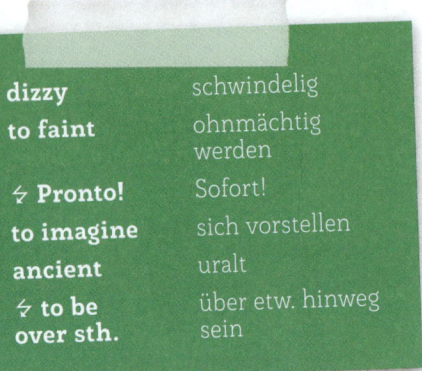

dizzy	schwindelig
to faint	ohnmächtig werden
⚡ **Pronto!**	Sofort!
to imagine	sich vorstellen
ancient	uralt
⚡ **to be over sth.**	über etw. hinweg sein

That's a lie, Katy thinks. Nothing is OK. Jeremy...

Katie feels **dizzy.** She can't breathe. And then, Katie **faints**.

The rescuer shouts, "Get a stretcher over here and some oxygen! **Pronto**! I think we're losing another one!" And then the woman is shouting at Katie.

"Come on sweetheart. Wake up! Keep fighting!"

8:50 a.m. Colby's Resort, Merimbula

"Ah, Stuart, you know how women... I mean people, **imagine** things," Frank says. "And about that missing wallet and jewellery. Stealing is nothing new here at Colby's. Remember when you stole Ellen from me, mate?"

"I'm not your mate, Frank – and I didn't 'steal' Ellen from you. I met her first! What are you..."

"Whatever, Stuart. It's **ancient** history. **I'm over it**. Anyway, stealing is just a part of life here. I mean, there are a few Aborigines... sorry, *Aboriginal Australian people* working here. So, what do you expect? Everyone knows they..."

Before Frank can finish his racist comment, Stuart jumps out of his chair.

He shouts, "You damned racist, Frank!"

And then, he loses control. He punches Frank on the nose – hard.

The telephone on Stuart's new desk rings.

"You'll pay for that, you damned Pommy," Frank shouts,

punching Stuart back. And then the two men start to fight, punching and shouting, until suddenly, the office door flies open.

wipe	wischen
to howl	jaulen

"Stop it! Stop it!" Beth shouts.
Tears are pouring down her face.
The phone on the desk is still ringing.
"Stuart! Oh Stuart!" Beth cries out.
"Beth! What's wrong? What's happened? Beth, tell me!"
But Beth cannot. She's in shock.
Frank answers the phone.
"McCabe's Resort, hello?" Frank listens and **wipes** some blood off his nose with a hand. Then he says, "Stuart? This call is for you. It's... It's the police."

Stuart walks in slowmotion to the phone. He hears Matilda outside. She's barking. Whining. **Howling.**
Silently, Frank gives Stuart the phone.
He says "Hello? Stuart Styles speaking."
Then he listens.
And then, Stuart's new nightmare begins.

7 Prayers, Comfort, Truth

9:05 a.m., the coastal road between Merimbula and Bega
Des's old jeep is travelling fast along the coastal road. There is a lot of traffic. But there is a police car in front of the jeep. Its siren is **blaring** loudly, as is the radio in Des's old jeep.

Exercise 14: Missing words.

Keep reading and complete the traffic report with the missing words in English!

> Unfall   Lastwagen   Rettungskräfte   Kinder   Berichte
> Schnellstraße   Familien   Kängurus   Richtungen

"The Princes 1. _Highway_ is closed in both 2. _detick_

There has been a **serious** 3. _accenting_. A school bus

and a 4. _truck_ have crashed. There are 5. _report_

that 6. _Kangoovus_ were on the road. Police and

7. _____ are at the scene. Many school

8. _____ are badly **injured**. Our **prayers** are with

them and their 9. _____."

"Please turn the damned radio off, Stuart," Beth says. "I can't **bear** it."

She is sitting next to him. She's silently praying: "Please let them live. Please don't let them be injured."

Stuart is not praying.

He's driving – fast but carefully.

He is **repeating** to himself: "Concentrate! No more accidents! The children need me. They cannot die. I could not bear it!"

coastal	an der Küste gelegen
to blare	*hier:* heulen
serious	ernst(haft)
injured	verletzt
prayers	Gebete
to bear sth.	etw. ertragen
to repeat	wiederholen

And Matilda? She is not whining anymore. She is sitting at Beth's feet. When she saw Beth and Stuart run to the jeep, she followed them. Her people have finally listened!

When Beth opened the jeep's door, Matilda jumped inside. She would not get out and Beth could not move her. As Des said in his will:

Wiederholung. **it's** und **its** werden häufig verwechselt – auch von Muttersprachlern!

it's = **it is** *(= es ist)* – der Apostroph steht für das fehlende ‚i';

its ist ein Possessivpronomen, d. h. es bezeichnet Besitz(tum), z. B. *Its siren is blaring loudly. = Seine Sirene (die des Jeeps) heult laut auf.*

she's a special dog. She's an Australian Shepherd 💡!

And right now, Matilda senses something new. She is **sniffing** the air. It smells like hope. It smells like answered prayers.

"Stuart?" Beth whispers. "The children are going to be OK. I... I know it. Or at least, Matilda knows it. Des always said she 'knows things'."

At the sound of her name, Matilda barks softly. Stuart doesn't answer. Beth sighs and looks at him.

"We have to talk about Des, Stuart. And about him and me – and about us. About, well, family. We have to..."

"I'm driving, Beth," Stuart says. "This really isn't the time to talk."

Stuart's voice is not rude, but soft and gentle. "We can talk after... after we know that the children are OK. I guess, I

Australian Shepherds kommen trotz ihres Namens nicht aus Australien, sondern aus Nordamerika. Australien Shepherds sind eine mittel-große, sehr intelligente Hunderasse. Sie wurden als Arbeitstiere bei der Hirtenarbeit eingesetzt und zeichnen sich durch sehr loyales Verhalten ihrem Herrchen gegenüber aus. Ebenso haben sie einen ausgeprägten Beschützertrieb sowie ein unbändiges Temperament. Sie können aber auch sehr eigenwillig sein.

Exercise 15: What time is it?

Look at the pictures and choose which sentence correctly tells the time!

1.

2.

a) It's a quarter to eight o'clock.

b) It's a quarter to eight p.m. ✗

a) It's two o'clock. ✗

b) It's two hour.

3.

4.

a) It's thirty to three.

b) It's three-thirty. ✗

a) It's five past twelve. ✗

b) It's twelve o'clock five.

to need surgery	operiert werden müssen
hallway	Flur
emergency room	Notaufnahme
crowded	voll (mit Leuten)

hope…" Stuart feels tears coming into his eyes.

"It's OK," Beth says. "You drive. I'll pray. We will talk, though. But you are right. Later."

10:05 a.m., Bega Hospital

"Later" comes very fast – much sooner than Beth or Stuart expected it to.

"Mr Styles?" a doctor says to Stuart. "I'm Dr Tammy Wells. I'm sorry to tell you this, but your son, Jeremy, **needs surgery** immediately." Dr Wells looks very worried. She is talking with Stuart and Beth at the hospital. They are in a **hallway** next to the **emergency room**. Many other worried parents and grandparents are there, too. It's loud and **crowded**. Some people are crying.

"Jeremy's injuries are very serious," Dr Wells continues. "And he's lost a lot of blood. That's a serious problem because of his blood type. He is Rh_{null} and that is very rare. We…"

Es gibt vier **Blutgruppen** (= **blood types**): A, B, AB und 0. Sie sind genetisch bestimmt und werden durch verschiedene Merkmale, z. B. Rhesusfaktor (Rh) weiter differenziert. Beim Blutspenden (= **blood donation**) ist eine Übereinstimmung der Blutgruppen für den Empfänger lebenswichtig. Bei Menschen mit sehr seltenen Blutgruppen ist es besonders schwer, einen passenden Spender (= **donor**) zu finden.

"I know, doctor," Stuart interrupts. He knows what information Dr Wells needs. And every second counts! "I'm not Rh_{null}, and Jeremy's sister isn't either."

"Yes, I know. We've already tested Katie's blood." Dr Wells sees Stuart's and Beth's faces and says, "Ka-

coincidence	Zufall
bruise	Bluterguss
minor	Minderjährige(r)
amazing	erstaunlich
birth mother	leibliche Mutter
to rub	reiben

tie will be OK. You can see her soon. But Jeremy..." Dr Wells turns to Beth. "Mrs. Jackson, your granddaughter is blood type Rh_{null}, too. Did you know that?" Dr Wells thinks this is a very lucky **coincidence**. It's almost a miracle.

"But there is another problem," she says. "Keira has lost blood, too. Don't worry, Mrs Jackson. It isn't serious. And Keira *could* even still donate blood. But she has a broken arm, some serious cuts, and lots of **bruises**. And since Keira is a **minor**, we..."

"I'll be the donor," Beth interrupts. "I'm Rh_{null}, too."

"Really?" Dr Wells exclaims. "That's fabulous. What an **amazing** coincidence!"

"Not really," Beth tells the doctor. But she is looking closely at Stuart. And then, Beth tells the truth.

"I'm Stuart's **birth mother**. Jeremy is my grandson."

"Oh." says the doctor. "So that means..."

"It's a long story, Dr Wells," Beth interrupts again. "Now about my grandson, Jeremy. He needs blood now. My blood."

"Of course! Come with me. Mr Styles, wait here. I'll..."

Dr Wells suddenly stops talking. She **rubs** her eyes. She wonders if she is seeing things. She's not.

"What on earth...?!" she exclaims. "How did that dog get in here? They're not **allowed** in hospital!"

But Matilda is not a dog to follow the **rules**. She is running down the hallway and barking. She's looking for Jeremy.

allowed	erlaubt
rule	Regel
needle	Nadel

"Matilda! Come here right now!" Stuart calls out. "Dr Wells, I'll take care of the dog. She's... she's part of our family. Please, you just take care of my son! And Beth?"

Stuart adds softly. "I... I don't know how to thank you... I just..."

"You don't have to thank me, Stuart. We'll talk later."

Minutes later, Nurse Tina Wong is with Beth in a small room. Nurse Wong puts a **needle** in Beth's arm. Beth has tears in her eyes.

"Does it hurt, Mrs Jackson?" the nurse asks.

Beth shakes her head and whispers "No."

She doesn't feel the needle.

Beth is seeing ghosts. And remembering another pain – a past pain. She sees herself at Short Point Beach, many years before.

Exercise 16: Spot the mistakes.

Keep reading and find the nine grammar and spelling mistakes. Then correct them!

Beth is only 15 year old, and she's with Des. He's 16 and so cool. He's also gorgeous, and so a sweetheart. They be surfing – riding the waves at Short Point. Beth is more fast than Des. She reaches the shore first and waves at him. He waves back and do a handstand. Then he wipes out and Beth laughs cause he looks so funny – and he's not hurt. Then Des is on the shore, to. He kisses her gentle on the lips. His lips are salty. So are hers.

The movie in Beth's head fast-forwards. She and Des are sneaking into Des bedroom. Its the same room Jeremy has now, Beth thinks. Oh Jeremy!

1. _____

2. _____

3. _____

4. _____

5. _____

6. _____

7. _____

8. _____

9. _____

passionately	leidenschaftlich
to be crazy about sb.	verrückt nach jmd. sein
careless	unvorsichtig, leichtsinnig
birth control	Verhütung
pregnant	schwanger
law	Gesetz
ward	Krankenhausstation

"How much longer will it take?" Beth asks Nurse Wong.

"About five more minutes. Are you OK? Do you feel faint?" Nurse Wong asks. She sounds worried.

"I'm fine," Beth says. "I'm just... remembering..."

Des's room. He's kissing Beth again and now she's kissing him, too. **Passionately**.

"So young," Beth whispers, and Nurse Wong looks at her. But Beth doesn't notice. She is lost in the past.

We were so **crazy about** each other, Beth thinks. But so stupid and **careless**, too. No condom. No **birth control**. And then, Beth is **pregnant**. But what should they do? The **law** says they can't get married. Beth is too young. She is also an Aboriginal Australian, and Des is white. The law won't even let them keep the baby! It's still the time of the "Stolen Generation 💡" in Australia.

And Beth? She loves Des, but she is not ready to be a mother! Beth wants to finish high school. Maybe become a professional surfer! She's good – even better than Des! Or maybe... maybe she will go to university to study business...

"Mrs Jackson? It's done," Nurse Wong says. "You need to rest for a few minutes. Here, drink this juice. Then, you can see your granddaughter. Jeremy is going into surgery now. But don't worry. He's in great hands. Dr Wells is the best!"

Beth sips her juice slowly. I did the right thing, she tells herself. And suddenly, she sees more ghosts. Mark and Susan Styles – a wonderful couple from Bournemouth. Professional surfers. They come every year to Colby's to surf at Short Point. They want to have a baby, but they can't. Susan cannot get pregnant.

But I could, Beth thinks. And what's worse, I was pregnant with a baby I could not keep – was not *allowed to* keep! Another ghost... Stuart's. It reminds Beth of now and where they are. She finishes her juice and stands up.

"Thank you, Nurse Wong. I feel OK. I just need to see my granddaughter... I mean my *granddaughters*. Can you please show me the **ward** where Keira and Katie are?"

"Of course, Mrs Jackson," Nurse Wong says. "Actually, they are in the same room. Another girl from Merimbula is there, too. Grace Amis."

Beth and Nurse Wong walk through the hospital's crowded

Kinder, die von australischen Ureinwohnern und „weißen" Partnern gezeugt wurden, wurden von der australischen Reglerung in den Jahren 1900 bis 1970 den Eltern weggenommen. Diese unmenschliche Praxis betraf 10 bis 30 % aller Kinder der australischen Ureinwohner. Viele wurden dadurch langfristig traumatisiert. Man bezeichnet diese Kinder als die **Stolen Generation** (= die gestohlene Generation). In dem Film *Rabbit Proof Fence* (deutscher Titel: *Der lange Weg nach Hause*) von Phillip Noyce wird dieses Drama anschaulich dargestellt (Achtung: FSK 12 Jahre).

Exercise 17: Relationships.

Who is who in *Danger Down Under*? Use the clues to find the solution word!

1. Des's son is ____.   ☐ _ _ _ _ _

2. ____ is Grandpa Mark's wife.   _ ☐ _ _ _

3. Beth's grandson is ____.   _ _ ☐ _ _ _

4. ____ is Des's nephew.   ☐ _ _ _ _

5. The very special dog is ____.   _ _ _ ☐ _ _ _

6. Stuart's wife was ____ .   _ _ _ _ ☐

7. Mike's sister is ____.   ☐ _ _ _ _

Solution word:

_ _ _ _ _ _ _

hallways. But Beth doesn't need the nurse to show her where the girls are. Beth – and Nurse Wong – suddenly hear barking. Loud, happy, barking. It's Matilda. She has **run away from** Stuart. She's found the girls first. Beth hears Katie cry out, "Oh Matilda! I'm so glad you're here!"

to run away (from)	abhauen (von)
to curse	(ver-)fluchen
relative	Verwandte(r)
to brake	bremsen
to swear	*hier:* schwören

12:00 p.m., coastal road, direction Melbourne.

Frank Morris is driving fast along the coastal road. He's driving towards Melbourne – and away from Colby's. Frank is angry. Very angry. And dangerous.

"Damn you Des!" he **curses** out loud. "*I* should have been your heir, Des. *I'm* your nephew! Your closest, legal **relative**!" Frank curses again. "And damn you too, Stuart!"

Suddenly, Frank realizes there is a slow truck in front of him. He has to **brake** hard. He's just in time. Franks tells himself to calm down. Drive carefully. No more accidents.

"I *will* make Stuart pay for this," he **swears**. "But later."

Epilogue

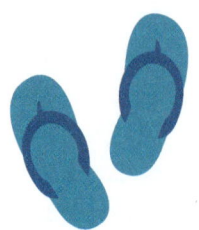

January, Short Point Beach, Summer in NSW Australia

The sun is shining on the waves at Short Point Beach on the Tasman Sea. The beach is full. It is a beautiful summer day. The waves are perfect for surfing.

"Are you ready, son?" Stuart asks Jeremy.

"Almost, Dad! I want to see Granny Beth take that wave first! And look at Grandma Susan! Wow! Dad, do you see her?" Jeremy is laughing. "I've got two surfer grannies, Dad. But Mum... Mum was better."

For a moment, Jeremy thinks he sees her, his mum, out on the sea. She's paddling on her surfboard, waiting for the next wave... like a ghost. And she waves at him and calls, "Jeremy! Come on!"

But it isn't his mum. And it isn't a ghost, either. It's Katie. She's with Mike. They are testing a school project. Something to do with surfboards and **tidal energy** 💡.

"Do you understand their project, Dad?" Jeremy asks.

"Not really, son." Stuart answers, and he smiles. He's happy. "But I'm glad Katie and Mike are working on it."

"I'm glad, too, Dad. Maybe I'll get involved in it when school starts next week. I'm glad I can finally go back to school."

"Well, learning from home wasn't so bad, was it? Grace and Keira visited you every day, right? And now, you're healthy again. All your injuries are **healed**."

"Yeah, I guess so. It's just... I still dream about it. The accident..." And just for a second, Jeremy sees the bus, the kangaroos, the truck... He hears Katie screaming,

tidal energy	Gezeitenenergie
to heal	heilen
to fade	verblassen
to growl	knurren

"Keep fighting, Jeremy! Don't give up!'"

"Well, that's normal, Jeremy," Stuart says. "It will **fade** with time. And well, Katie, she..."

"She saved my life. I know." Jeremy shakes his head. "So it's a good thing she learnt CPR, right?"

Matilda barks. She's sitting at Jeremy's feet. He smiles at her and scratches her behind the ears.

"Right, Matilda. Let's go!" he tells, her. "And, Dad, you too!" Jeremy picks up his surfboard and Stuart takes his, too.

Matilda follows them to the water. She watches "her boy" swim out without her. Then suddenly, she **growls**. She smells danger in the air.

Lust auf einen weiteren Schüler-Lernkrimi? In *Students Undercover* findest du weitere Informationen über das Umweltprojekt mit Gezeitenenergie von Mike (ISBN 978-3-8174-4258-4).
Lies nach, was auf der Schüler-Klimakonferenz in London passiert.

Up above Short Point, Frank Morris is looking through his binoculars. He's watching Stuart and his family. And Frank whispers, "It's later Stuart. Later is today."
And then, Frank hears barking. Very loud barking...

Final Check

Answers

Glossary

List of Exercises

Final Check

Exercise 1: School uniforms.

What do kids wear to school in Australia? Label the parts of the school uniforms!

1. Skirt

2. Shirt

3. Polo Shirt

4. trousers/shorts

5. trousers/shorts

Exercise 2: Who is it?

Write the name(s) of the *Danger Down Under* character(s) next to their descriptions!

1. Ate sweets to comfort himself in the UK:

Jeremy

2. Loved only one woman his whole life:

Desmond

3. Heirs to Colby's Resort:

Jeremy, Stuart, Caitic

4. Whines, howls and growls!

5. An Aboriginal Australian and resort manager:

6. An angry racist who curses a lot:

7. Was mean, cold and rude to Jeremy:

Eva

Exercise 3: Synonyms.

Match up the words with the same or similar meanings!

1. f hurt   **a)** unbelievable

2. e in fact   **b)** softly

3. a amazing   **c)** immediately

4. c pronto   **d)** blame

5. d fault   **e)** actually

6. b gently   **f)** painful

Exercise 4: Katie's journal.

Katie's journal entry is missing its verbs. Put the verbs in the right place in the simple past!

go   have   think   help   see   laugh   catch   seem

wipe out

At first, we **1.** _have_ a fabulous time at South Point today. I

2. _____ Mike with his tidal energy project (cool!) and then

we **3.** _cat_ some great waves. So funny when Mike

4. _____! Even Jeremy **5.** _____. He **6.** _went_

surfing again, too! He seems to be getting over his trauma

about mum. At least, I **7.** _____ he **8.** _____ lots better!

But then Matilda **9.** _____ something. She…

Sorry dear journal. Mike's here! We have been…

Exercise 5: Odd one out.

Which word doesn't fit with the others? Underline the odd one out!

1. strange   weird   bizarre   unfair

2. cry out   shout   exclaim   sulk

3. nurse   coincidence   ward   surgery

4. manager   boss   chef   employee

5. stretcher   grave   die   ghost

Exercise 6: Confusing words!

**Underline the right word to complete the definition.
(Remember: Spelling counts!)**

1. Jeremy expects / ~~excepts~~ to hate Australia.

2. The Styles family are Des's ~~hairs~~ / heirs .

3. Beth says she can't ~~bare~~ / bear listening to the radio report.

4. The dog is wagging ~~its~~ / it's tail.

5. Stuart doesn't ~~lie~~ / lie , but he doesn't tell the ~~whole~~ / hole truth.   *whole*

6. After the accident, Katie felt dizzy and couldn't breath /
breathe .

Exercise 7: Australia.

**Use the clues to help you find the eight hidden words about
Australia and write the words next to the clues.**

1. Hello! _____   **5.** a marsupial _____

2. Australia _____   **6.** breakfast _____

3. kiss _____   **7.** afternoon _____

4. a highway _____   **8.** food _____

T	H	G'	D	A	Y	R	T	P	K
U	A	A	U	S	S	I	E	R	O
R	V	B	C	M	I	Q	L	I	A
B	R	E	K	K	Y	U	T	N	L
S	O	T	E	O	D	N	I	C	A
D	A	S	R	T	U	C	K	E	R
O	P	A	S	H	A	Z	U	S	G

Answers

Exercise 1:   **1.** stands up **2.** walk **3.** doesn't open **4.** stand
5. be **6.** sees **7.** is **8.** Can

Exercise 2:   **1.** c **2.** g **3.** a **4.** f **5.** b **6.** d **7.** e

Exercise 3:   **1.** so **2.** much **3.** such **4.** best **5.** so **6.** many
7. than **8.** some

Exercise 4:   **1.** didn't know **2.** had **3.** knew **4.** was
5. visited **6.** learned **7.** were

Exercise 5:   **1.** e **2.** d **3.** a **4.** b **5.** c

Exercise 6:   **1.** instead **2.** front **3.** opposite **4.** wall/walls
5. photo

Exercise 7:   **1.** earth **2.** shore **3.** sweetheart **4.** journal
5. part-time **6.** sparkling

Exercise 8:   **1.** inside **2.** since **3.** already **4.** again **5.** too
6. just **7.** so **8.** else

Exercise 9:   **1.** she **2.** him **3.** her **4.** their **5.** his **6.** them
7. her **8.** me **9.** he

Exercise 10: **1.** have **2.** has **3.** has **4.** have **5.** has **6.** have

Exercise 11: **1.** unfriendly **2.** nervous **3.** furious
4. ashamed

Exercise 12: **1.** quickly **2.** slowly **3.** fast **4.** easy **5.** carefully
6. dangerous **7.** extremely **8.** slow
9. strange

Exercise 13: 1. rescue workers 2. stretcher 3. ambulance 4. electronic devices 5. wallet

Exercise 14: 1. Highway 2. directions 3. accident 4. truck/ lorry 5. reports 6. kangaroos 7. rescue workers 8. children 9. families

Exercise 15: 1. b 2. a. 3. b. 4. a

Exercise 16: 1. year → years 2. so → such 3. be → are 4. more fast → faster 5. do → does 6. cause → because 7. to → too 8. gentle → gently 9. Its → It's

Exercise 17: 1. Stuart 2. Susan 3. Jeremy 4. Frank 5. Matilda 6. Ellen 7. Grace
Solution word: Surfing

Final Check

Exercise 1: 1. blazer 2. skirt 3. shirt 4. shorts 5. trousers

Exercise 2: 1. Jeremy 2. Des/Desmond (Colby) 3. Stuart, Katie, Jeremy 4. Matilda 5. Beth 6. Frank 7. Keira

Exercise 3: 1. f 2. e 3. a 4. c. 5. d. 6. b

Exercise 4: 1. had 2. helped 3. caught 4. wiped out 5. laughed 6. went 7. thought 8. seemed 9. saw

Exercise 5: **1.** unfair **2.** sulk **3.** inheritance **4.** chef **5.** stretcher

Exercise 6: **1.** expects **2.** heirs **3.** bear **4.** signs **5.** lie, whole **6.** breathe

Exercise 7: **1.** g'day **2.** Aussie **3.** pash **4.** Princes **5.** koala **6.** brekky **7.** avro **8.** Tucker

T	H	G'	D	A	Y	R	T	P	K
U	A	A	U	S	S	I	E	R	O
R	V	B	C	M	I	Q	L	I	A
B	R	E	K	K	Y	U	T	N	L
S	O	T	E	O	D	N	I	C	A
D	A	S	R	T	U	C	K	E	R
O	P	A	S	H	A	Z	U	S	G

Glossary

⚡	= umgangssprachlich
pl	= Plural

accident	Unfall
actually	tatsächlich, eigentlich
allowed	erlaubt
already	bereits, schon
amazing	erstaunlich, unglaublich
ancient	uralt
ashamed	beschämt
to bark	bellen
to be crazy about sb.	verrückt nach jmd. sein
to be mad at sb.	auf jmd. wütend/ärgerlich sein
⚡ to be over sth.	über etw. hinweg sein
to be to blame	an etw. schuld sein
to bear sth.	etw. ertragen
to behave	sich verhalten
binoculars pl.	Fernglas
birth control	Verhütung
birth mother	leibliche Mutter

bizarre	seltsam, wunderlich
to blare	*hier:* heulen, plärren
to brake	bremsen
to breathe	atmen
bruise	Bluterguss
to bury	begraben
busy	beschäftigt
cancer	Krebs (Krankheit)
careless	unvorsichtig, leichtsinnig
to change the subject	das Thema wechseln
cheek	Wange
closely	genau, nah
coastal	an der Küste gelegen
coincidence	Zufall
to comfort	trösten
to complain	sich beschweren
condition	Bedingung
to continue	weitermachen, hier: weiterreden
CPR (Cardiopulmonary Resuscitation)	Herz-Lungen-Wiederbelebung, Reanimation
crowded	voll (mit Leuten)
cruel	grausam
crunchy	knusprig
to cry out	aufschreien, laut rufen

to curse	(ver-)fluchen
ϟ Damn you!	Scher dich zum Teufel!
day-to-day	alltäglich
dear	Schatz, Liebling
delicious	lecker
devices	Geräte
dizzy	schwindelig
eavesdropping	Lauschen
emergency room	Notaufnahme
employee	Angestellte(r)
except	außer
exciting	aufregend
to expect	erwarten
experienced	erfahren
to explain	erklären
facilities manager	Hausmeister
to fade	verblassen
to faint	ohnmächtig werden
fault	Schuld
female	weiblich
finally	endlich
ϟ to fire sb.	jmd. entlassen, feuern
to follow	folgen
to forgive	vergeben
frantically	hektisch

to frown	die Stirn runzeln
gently	sanft
to get in trouble	Ärger kriegen
⚡ to get the message	kapieren, verstehen
ghost	Gespenst, Geist
to giggle	kichern
glad	froh
gorgeous	sehr attraktiv (Mensch), sehr schön (Landschaft)
grave	Grab
to growl	knurren
hallway	Flur
⚡ to hang out with sb.	mit jmd. abhängen
⚡ to have a crush on sb.	in jdn. verknallt sein, auf jmd. stehen
to heal	heilen
heirs pl.	Erben
to howl	jaulen
to hug	umarmen
huge	riesig
to hurt (hurt, hurt) sb.	jmd. wehtun
to imagine	sich vorstellen
in fact	und zwar
inheritance	Erbe
injured	verletzt

instead	stattdessen
to interrupt	unterbrechen
jewellery	Schmuck
journal	Tagebuch
to jump up	aufspringen
just beyond	direkt dahinter
⚡ Just get on with it!	Mach einfach!
Keep fighting!	Kämpf weiter!
law	Gesetz
to leave (left, left) sb. alone	jmd. in Ruhe lassen
lick	lecken
lie	Lüge
to look sth. up	etw. nachschlagen
to lose weight	(Gewicht) abnehmen
mean	gemein, fies
minor	Minderjährige(r)
to move	*hier:* umziehen
to need surgery	operiert werden müssen
needle	Nadel
⚡ Never mind!	Macht nix! Was soll's!
nevertheless	nichtsdestotrotz
nightmare	Alptraum
to notice	(be-)merken
⚡ Oh well...	Tja...

opposite	gegenüber
overweight	übergewichtig
owner	Besitzer
oxygen	Sauerstoff
painful	schmerzhaft
part-time	Teilzeit
passionately	leidenschaftlich
polite	höflich
to pour	fließen, ausgießen
prayers	Gebete
pregnant	schwanger
⚡ Pronto!	Sofort!
to punch	schlagen
to reach	erreichen
to realize	realisieren, wahrnehmen
recently	in letzter Zeit, neuerdings
recipe	(Koch)rezept
reincarnation	Wiedergeburt
relative	Verwandte(r)
to repeat	wiederholen
⚡ right on cue	wie gerufen
to rub	reiben
rudely	unhöflich
rule	Regel
to run (ran, run) sth.	etw. führen, betreiben

to run away (from)	abhauen (von)
to save	retten
to scratch	kratzen
to scream	schreien
secretly	heimlich
to seem	erscheinen
to sense	spüren, ahnen
serious	ernst(haft)
to shake	*hier:* zittern
shore	Ufer, Küste
⚡ to show sb. the ropes	jdn. mit allem vertraut machen
to sigh	seufzen
to sign	unterschreiben
to sip	nippen
to slam	zuknallen, zuschlagen
to sneak around	(herum)schleichen
to sniff	*hier:* wittern
solution	Lösung
sparkling	glitzernd
special	besonders
to start over	neu anfangen
to steer	lenken
⚡ to stick up for sb.	für jmd. eintreten
sticky	klebrig

strange	komisch, ungewohnt
stretcher	Trage, Bahre
suddenly	plötzlich
to sulk	schmollen
sure	sicher
to swear	*hier:* schwören
sweetheart	Süße(r), Schatz
to take (took, taken) care of sb.	sich um jmd. kümmern
tear	Träne
to tell the truth	die Wahrheit sagen
⚡ That's his business!	Das geht mich nichts an!
though	*hier:* aber, jedoch
tidal energy	Gezeitenenergie
to tip sb. off	jdn. warnen, jdm. einen Hinweis geben
truck	Lastwagen
unbelievable	unglaublich
unhealthy	ungesund
upset	aufgebracht, verärgert
voice	Stimme
to wag (a tail)	(mit dem Schwanz) wedeln
wallet	Brieftasche
ward	Krankenhausstation
⚡ Watch out!	Pass auf!

weird	seltsam, komisch
⚡ **weirdo**	Spinner
⚡ **What on earth...?!**	Was zum Teufel ...?!
to whine	winseln
to whisper	flüstern
whole	ganz
will	Testament
wipe	wischen
worried	besorgt

List of Exercises

	Focus	Exercise	Page
1	Grammar	Missing verbs	8
2	Comprehension	Chronology	11
3	Grammar	How much?	16
4	Grammar	The past	19
5	Vocabulary	Matching	21
6	Comprehension	Katie's room?	25
7	Vocabulary	Fill in the gaps	28
8	Vocabulary	Useful adverbs	30
9	Grammar	Pronouns	35
10	Grammar	Present perfect	40
11	Vocabulary	How people behave	42
12	Grammar	Adjective or adverb?	45
13	Vocabulary	Fill in the gaps	53
14	Vocabulary	Missing words	56
15	Vocabulary	What time is it?	59
16	Grammar	Spot the mistakes	63
17	Comprehension	Relationships	66

Bildnachweis

Shutterstock: Glühbirne: vectorplus (ganzes Buch), 6: Andy Frith; 7: Golden Sikorka; 8: Andy Frith; 10: Yefym Turkin; 13: kateukraine, 14. ikonim; 16: POKPAK101; 18: Andy Frith; 21: Jordi Fernandez Ventura (Panda) Andy Frith (Känguru), Ra_sveta (Schafe); Jovanovic Dejan (Smiley), Sky-iris (Katze); 22: Weredragon; 23: Ekaterina Glazkova (Schüler), Andy Frith (Schildkröte); 24: Pixel Shot; 25: keko_ka; 26: Andy Frith; 29: FOXARTBOX; 31: AnnstasAg; 32: Elena Nayashkova; 34: Dukesn; 35: FOXARTBOX; 37: Anastasiia Sarana; 39: LydiaLyd; 42: GoodStudio; 43: Oleg7799; 44-45: dimensi_design; 46: kwest; 47: Annareichel; 48, 50: FOXARTBOX; 51: Kochkanyan Juliya; 53: Simply Amazing (Krankenwagen), Mind Pixell (Bus) ; 55: Malysh Falko; 58: Foxartbox; 59: ai_stock (3.), Morphart Creation (4.) wilkastok (1., 2.); 62: Qualit Design; 66: Tartila; 68: Andy Frith; 70: portumen; 72: Batsheys; 75: GoodStudios

Creativemarket: Klebestreifen: patternpop studio (ganzes Buch).

Notizen

Spannend Sprachen lernen

ISBN 978-3-8174-1655-4

› spannende Comics für die Niveaus A1 und A2
› landestypische Settings, authentische Sprache
› Übungen nach jeder Geschichte
› Vokabelangaben auf jeder Seite
› Online-Vokabeltraining mit phase6

ISBN 978-3-8174-1996-8

www.circonverlag.de